The Elementary Teacher's Communication Guide

Third Edition

Karin-Leigh Spicer
Wright State University

KENDALL/HUNT PUBLISHING COMPANY
4050 Westmark Drive   Dubuque, Iowa 52002

Apple cover image illustrated by Jeannette M. Spicer
Background cover image © 2003 Artville

Contents

Communication Model 51

Model 52

Communication Activities for Students 53

Minute Activities 55

Parent-Teacher Conferences 62

Activities 64

Preface

The purpose of this guide is to give the elementary school teacher basic guidelines for the use of good communication skills in the classroom. Over the course of a school year, teachers have the opportunity to guide and shape young learners. Utilizing good communication skills is essential for teachers to pass on their knowledge to their students.

This guide is divided into eight sections: oral communication skills, nonverbal communication skills, story delivery skills, writing skills, addressing communication, communication model, communication activities, parent teacher conferences. In the first section, oral communication skill, how an elementary school teacher talks to his/her students is discussed. Why vocal projection, rate of speed, pitch, inflection, and language usage have an impact on the level of student interest and understanding are examined. Discussion in the nonverbal communication section concentrates on how teachers can effectively use eye contact, body movement, facial expressions, and visual aids in the classroom. The third section, story delivery skills, explains step by step how to read and tell stories to children.

The writing skills section offers guidance on how to organize written messages to administration, faculty and parents. This section is not meant to be a substitute for a comprehensive business style writing course but rather to offer practical ideas on ways to facilitate effective written communication appropriate for the elementary educator. The fifth section presents nine teachers' ideas on the importance of communication in the classroom. The sixth section presents a communication model. This is a visual representation of communication in the classroom.

The communication activities sections offers simple, fun and quick activities for teachers to use in the classroom. The final section, parent-teacher conferences presents suggestions for setting up conferences.

Oral Communication Skills

In a single school day you will lecture, read, explain, discuss, negotiate, encourage, praise, and discipline your students. Oral communication is how you present yourself through speaking. It is *how* you say something. Young learners will form impressions not only on the content of the message but on *how* the message was delivered. When you have good oral communication skills you will be more effective in delivering the desired message to your students.

It is not difficult to improve your speaking skills. The first step is recognizing your strengths and weaknesses. Can all your students hear me? Do your students ask you to repeat information frequently? Do you speak too fast? Do you pronounce words correctly? Are your students easily bored during class discussions? Do you lecture in a monotone or are you expressive and interesting? The more you are aware of what you do in the classroom the easier it will be to assess your speaking skills.

The second step, improving your speaking skills, largely depends on motivation. How much time are you willing to spend on improving or learning new skills? Just as you tell your students to give one hundred percent of their effort, learning good communication skills will take one hundred percent of your effort. The key word is "motivation."

To discover what are good classroom speaking skills use the scale in **Activity 1** to evaluate fellow teachers' classroom speaking skills. Then use the scale to honestly evaluate your own speaking skills.

Vocal Projection

Simply stated, *all* students must be able to hear and understand you. By saying *all*, this includes not only those students sitting in front, but also those students who sit on the outer perimeter and in the back of the classroom. In a classroom, you must adapt your voice to meet the needs on an ever changing classroom environment. One way to ensure that students can hear and understand you is through vocal projection.

Vocal projection is a term used in communication to discuss the degree of loudness in a teacher's voice. Do students have to strain every inch of their bodies to hear you? Do students in the outer perimeter and in the back of the classroom seem to lose interest in class discussions more quickly than the students in the front? Do a majority of students consistently ask you to repeat statements? If the answer to any of these questions is yes, then vocal projection could be the source of the problem.

Many teachers fail to realize that their conversational voice (how loud they talk to another person or small group of people) is not adequate in speaking to a classroom of young learners. A classroom has many noise distractions: students crumbling and tearing paper, sharpening pencils, coughing, sneezing, and whispering, just to list a few. Outside noises also can distract a student's attention away from the teacher. Bells, buses, children on the playground, and announcements contribute to outside interferences. Your voice must be loud enough for students to hear the information you are presenting. Note, this does not mean using your lung capacity at full level (screaming). It simply means finding a level of vocal projection of which students can hear you comfortably (See **Activity 2**).

When students cannot hear, they become distracted and lose interest. Students can also feel uneasy and confused when they have not heard directions, comments, or descriptions concerning a particular topic, project, or assignment.

No human, adult or child, has the ability to listen to another human one hundred percent of the time. If you consciously project your voice so that all students can hear, noise distractions will be minimal. Good vocal projection will maximize the opportunity for efficient listening by all your young learners.

Rate of Speed

How fast can you say, "*He hails her hallowed highness*"? Usually as a teacher you will speak at a rate that is appropriate for the subject material. A fast rate can imply that the information is humorous, light or unimportant. A slow, more deliberate rate can mean that the information is serious, deep, or important. If you feel excited, happy, or energetic, you will probably speak at a much faster rate. Your rate of speed will be slower if you feel calm, tired or sad.

The rate of speed can also affect a student's understanding of the material presented. Young learners are capable of hearing words as fast as they are spoken. But they cannot always make sense of those words in the same short period of time. If you deliver a lecture quickly students may have a difficult time comprehending the lecture's meaning, especially if the material contains abstract or complex ideas. If the lecture is delivered too slowly students may lose interest in the material, as well as in you.

The rate of delivery must match the meaning and content of the subject material if any degree of learning is to take place in the classroom. When students are not given ample time to let new ideas sink in, they can become confused, stressed and disenchanted with the learning process. In the same vein, students can become just as disenchanted when subject material is repeated over and over and over again.

Many teachers forget that they have been teaching the same basic material for years. These teachers will *zip* through a lecture or assignment, failing to realize that this is new material to their students. Other teachers fail to understand that the classroom is comprised of students with different learning abilities. While one class may need more time to examine a particular concept, the next group may have little difficulty and quickly move to other material.

When examining your rate of speed consider two areas: first, the content of the subject and second, the learning abilities of your students. If you feel the material is complex or your students may have difficulty understanding it utilize *pauses*. This simply means pausing at the end of a difficult concept or idea and waiting at least five seconds (e.g., count to yourself one thousand one, one thousand two...) before moving to other material. Pauses allow young learners to grasp ideas, write down definitions, or ask questions.

Other techniques that help to slow your rate of speed include asking questions to see if your students understand the material, repeating definitions, and spelling new words. Examples and illustrations will also slow your rate of delivery of new material. Applying any of these techniques in your classroom allows young learners to catch material you may have said too quickly.

The easiest way to tell if you need to work on your rate of speed is to listen to your students. Do they continually ask that information be repeated, complain that you talk too fast, seem to lose interest in material, or become impatient during discussion? If so you may want to re-examine your rate of speed.

Pitch

Pitch is the highness or lowness of a sound. Pitch is subjective; it is determined by you or your student's judgment. The higher the frequency (number of vibrations that occur in a specific period of time), the higher the pitch; the lower the frequency, the lower the pitch. For many teachers pitch rises when they become excited, nervous, or frightened. But if they are bored, tired, or uninterested, their pitch lowers as they speak.

Your normal (habitual) pitch will usually cause no specific problems in the classroom environment. Unfortunately, teachers and students apply certain stereotypes to how an individual's voice should sound. For example, we assume men should have lower voices than women. We also assume that the smaller a person is physically, the higher the pitch will be.

A teacher using too high a pitch may have problems with student attention and discipline. A teacher using too low a pitch may find students uneasy and under undue stress in the classroom. The first teacher is labeled as *weak*, the latter is labeled as *authoritarian*.

As the teacher you will be talking for more of each day than your children. If you are using an unnatural pitch over the course of that day you may strain your vocal chords or temporarily lose your voice. Either condition can cause obvious problems in your classroom.

If you believe your pitch may be too high or too low you must first determine what your optimum (the pitch naturally produced by the vocal chords) pitch is (See **Activity 3**). After you discovered your optimum pitch you need to compare the two pitches (optimum and habitual) to see if they are the same (See **Activity 4**). The two pitches should be within two tones of each other. If you find a larger distance between the two pitches, you may want to consider working on changing the habitual pitch.

A change in your habitual pitch takes little more than practicing talking at your optimum pitch. Reading from newspapers, magazines, or books in your conversational voice will help you feel more comfortable with the new pitch. This type of practice allows you to hear when your voice has moved away from the optimum pitch.

Vocal Inflection

Two teachers tell the same story to a group of young learners. One teacher has students thoroughly enthralled with the story. The other teacher barely makes it to the middle of the story before students become bored, restless, and inattentive. The difference? One answer may be the ability to utilize vocal inflection.

Vocal inflection is the change in pitch that occurs when you put vocal emphasis on words you feel are important. Vocal inflection communicates your attitudes and feelings to your students (See **Activity 5**). It shows your interest in a subject, approval when a student has done well, displeasure over misbehavior, and seriousness in rules students must follow.

You can use vocal inflection to indicate doubt or uncertainty, ask questions (e.g., 1 + 1 = _____, blue and yellow make _____), or to emphasize important words or thoughts in a story. When you use vocal inflection, students know when sentences, paragraphs, or stories end. Through your use of vocal inflection young learners know when an idea or concept is important and pay more attention to names of places, people, and things discussed in class.

If you use little or no vocal inflection your communication is dry, lifeless, and boring. When you continuously speak in a monotone voice (e.g. the same level of pitch) young learners lose interest. In everyday conversations, most individuals use vocal inflection. Problems result when you omit vocal inflection when talking with your students. Many teachers believe to be considered *credible* they need to speak in a *teacher-like* manner. This belief has a direct outcome -- a monotone delivery. If you use this approach you will lose your students' interest, excitement, and curiosity. Limited vocal inflection in your voice demonstrates lack of interest in the subject you're discussing.

Listen to yourself. How do you express your feelings? How do you discuss topics? How do you tell a story? Do your students seem to lose interest in what you are talking about? When you use your voice to show excitement and enthusiasm about learning your young learners will take notice.

Language

The difficulty in discussing the problems associated with language usage in the classroom is that many teachers fail to recognize that problems exist. Students have a long formal process by which they learn to write in contrast to the casual and almost automatic way by which they learn to speak. Students spend years in the classroom studying and practicing how to write while their speaking skills develop through arbitrary means. Students are taught to depend on writing skills instead of speaking skills.

The first area you need to examine is how appropriate is your vocabulary to the grade level you are teaching. One can always find teachers who are experts in their chosen fields, but failures in the classroom. The jargon (technical language, e.g., medical or law terms) and vocabulary these teachers use is too difficult for their students to understand. What is the use of being an expert if you are unable to share that expertise with your children? If you are a sixth grade teacher, you do not use a vocabulary that only college students would understand.

A second area that causes problems is correct word pronunciation. It is common and easy to mispronounce words. We all do it. For example, *thinking* is pronounced *thinkin* (the "g" is dropped) and *wash* is pronounced *warsh* (the"r" is added). When a teacher pronounces these words incorrectly, students still know what is meant. The problem is that students learn from their teachers. If you mispronounce words, so will your students. You cannot assume or expect your students to have good pronunciation skills if you do not (See **Activity 6**).

The best way to eliminate the problem is to be consciously aware of your blatant mispronunciations. In the course of a day, one will unintentionally pronounce a word incorrectly -- teachers are not perfect. The point is to catch consistently mispronounced words. If you are going to be using words that you are unfamiliar with -- such as names of foreign leaders, countries, or science terms -- consult the dictionary or call the local library, newspaper, radio or television station for a correct pronunciation.

The usage of slang (i.e., words not accepted as formal language) in the classroom can also present problems for teachers. You, as well as your children, use slang in and outside the classroom. Slang can be used to lessen the formalities of verbal conversation and create bonds among a group. Slang can cause problems in the classroom if it is overused. (See **Activity 7**).

As a teacher you will need to use a vocabulary that establishes credibility and makes a distinction between you and your students. Many new teachers make the mistake of sounding more like a student than a teacher. This creates a problem in establishing credibility and authority. Remember, young learners will model their own language skills after their teacher.

Again the best way for you to determine if you have a problem with slang is to be consciously aware of your choice in language. What words do you use to express yourself to your children? How do your students react after you've made a comment? Can you make a list of the slang you use daily? How long is the list? Then make a concentrated effort to eliminate the words you feel are inappropriate from your vocabulary.

Activities

1. Use the following speaking scale to evaluate your own or a fellow teacher's overall oral communication skills. Mark the appropriate category.

Speaking Scale

	Needs Work	Average	Outstanding
Vocal projection	_____	_____	_____
Rate of speed	_____	_____	_____
Pitch	_____	_____	_____
Vocal inflection	_____	_____	_____
Language Usage	_____	_____	_____
Overall effectiveness	_____	_____	_____

After you have rated a teacher, can you give an example of a oral communication skill that s/he does well? One s/he does poorly? On what one skill would you have her/him work?

2. The following activities can help demonstrate how loudly or softly you are speaking.

A: Select a series of items -- numbers, letters, etc. Start saying them softly and increase your volume until you are speaking as loudly as you can without screaming or straining your voice. Repeat the exercise, only start speaking loudly and decrease the volume until you are almost whispering. Again, do not strain your voice.

B. Read aloud using whatever materials you prefer -- stories, news articles, etc. Have a friend sit across the room while you read the selections aloud. Make sure you project adequately so your friend can hear all parts of your material.

3. The following activities will help you locate your optimum pitch.

A. Sing the highest and lowest limits you can comfortably reach and then find those limits on the piano. Next, locate the middle of the range. In general, your optimum pitch should be about two notes below this middle point.

B. One other way to approximate your optimum pitch is to sing down the scale to the lowest note you can reach comfortably. Next, sing up again five notes to reach your optimum pitch.

4. The following activity will help you locate your habitual pitch.

Read aloud a passage from a magazine or book at a normal conversational loudness. Ask a friend to listen to you and to find the note on the piano that is closest to the average pitch of your reading. You may need to read the passage three or four times to make sure your pitch level is staying the same. The note closest to your average speaking level is your habitual pitch.

5. The following activities can help illustrate quickly and clearly the difference voice inflection can have upon your delivery.

A.   Say the word "oh" to mean:
>   Really?
>   I understand.
>   How revolting!
>   Interesting.
>   Me?

B.   Say the following sentence out loud emphasizing the word that is underlined.
>   <u>Yes</u>, she is very pretty.
>   Yes, <u>she</u> is very pretty.
>   Yes, she <u>is</u> very pretty.
>   Yes, she is <u>very</u> pretty.
>   Yes, she is very <u>pretty</u>.

C. Say the following sentences stressing the word underlined to mean the following:

I hope she will stay. (I feel this way)

I <u>hope</u> she will stay. (I an encouraged to believe)

I hope <u>she</u> will stay. (no one else is concerned)

I hope she <u>will</u> stay. (there is no doubt about the outcome)

I hope she will <u>stay</u>. (no question of leaving)

6. The following activities will help with word pronunciation and enunciation.

A. Pronounce the following set of words. Explain what each word means.

pen	pin
picture	pitcher
beg	big
wither	weather
ten	tin

B. See how fast you can say these tongue twisters.

Toy boat. Toy boat. Toy boat.

Sheep shouldn't sleep in a shack. Sheep should sleep in a shed.

I can't stand rotten writing when it's written rotten.

Cross crossings cautiously!

Round and round the rugged rocks the ragged rascal ran.

Make a list of your own.

B. Pronounce the following words.

our   (not)   are

just   (not)   jist

can't   (not)   kaint

Make a list of your own.

C.   Pronounce the following words.

going (not) goin'

walking (not) walkin'

talking (not) talkin'

nothing (not) nothin'

Make a list of your own.

7.   The following activity will demonstrate how much slang you know.
Explain each word or phrase.

A. Beige	B. Be-bop
C. Jocks	D. Fresh
E. Stay down	F. Z's
G. Rays	H. Burnt
I. Team Xerox	J. Homeboy/homegirl

Answers:

A. boring

B. 50's music

C. athletes

D. good, cool

E. be cool

F. sleep

G. sun

H. tired

I. cheat, copy

J. friend

Make a list of your own.

Nonverbal Communication Skills

Young learners are exposed to a multitude of non-verbal signals from the moment they enter your classroom. A smile, a wink, a hand wave, or a bulletin board all communicate nonverbal messages. Through nonverbal signals you can reinforce your verbal messages, giving additional meaning to what you say. Students will form impressions on the importance of your verbal messages through your nonverbal communication.

Many teachers fail to recognize their nonverbal behaviors and the impact these behaviors have in the classroom. Facial expressions, eye contact, and body movements are natural extensions of ourselves and the use of visual aids is a natural extension of teaching. Nonverbal communication is always present in your classroom. Do you roll your eyes when students give incorrect answers? Do you look away before a student has finished speaking? Do you slouch in your chair? Does your back face your students when you use the blackboard? Do you hold up a rock during a science lesson so that all your students can see it? What you do has a strong impact on the communicative atmosphere in your classroom. As a teacher you need to be aware of the nonverbal behaviors you commonly use and the meaning these behaviors convey.

Mixed messages can occur in the classroom when the nonverbal behavior differs from the verbal message. When this happens the nonverbal communication is believed more often than the verbal. The influence of nonverbal communication in the classroom is strong and lasting.

A student answers a question wrong. You verbally respond by praising the students for attempting to answer the question but your facial expression shows exasperation and displeasure. Because the verbal and nonverbal messages are different, the student ends up being confused and embarrassed. This student will think twice before answering your next question.

It is not difficult to improve your nonverbal skills. The more you are aware of your own nonverbal behaviors the better you will be able to use them successfully in your classroom.

To discover what are good classroom nonverbal skills use the scale in **Activity 1** to evaluate the nonverbal skills of fellow teachers. Then use the scale to honestly evaluate your own nonverbal skills.

Facial Expressions

The expressions on your face can send a wide range of nonverbal messages to your students. Facial expressions highlight many of the emotions you feel during school day -- from excitement to frustration.

Students need and want to know how you will react to them breaking rules, answering questions, laughing when something funny happens, whispering, and the like. Your young learners will learn how you feel primarily through your facial expressions. Facial expressions are the most common method of transmitting nonverbal messages to students.

Because your students will rely on your facial expressions to confirm your verbal messages, mixed signals can become a problem. As a teacher your facial expressions should be consistent with you verbal message. When you send mixed signals students become confused and distrustful of your verbal messages.

If you are expressionless you may also have problems with young learners. For students, it's as if they were asked to look into a blank wall. Students will look at your face for approval, interest, anger, and a variety of other reactions to their behaviors in the classroom.

When you tell your students, "Good job" or "You may talk among yourselves quietly," does your face confirm that verbal message? Or are you expressionless? Students will more often remember your facial signals or lack of expressiveness than the verbal message. If you use few facial expressions when talking to your young learners you will find them lacking interest or motivation in the topic.

Facial expressions are an innate part of your communication system. Though it is impossible to be aware of all your facial expressions at any given time you will have few problems if you are consistent, honest, and open with your students.

Eye Contact

Your eye contact plays a very important role in the classroom communication process. How often do you look at your students when you tell them a story? During a lecture? When you talk to them individually? The amount of time you maintain eye contact with your students generally indicates the degree and quality of that relationship. Eye contact shows your interest, concern, and awareness of the activities taking place in your classroom. It is always a powerful communicator.

If you constantly have your eyes buried in lecture notes or books, you will give students impressions of lack of preparedness and interest. If your eyes are glued to the blackboard or overhead projector you will fail to see raised hands, confused looks, and students squirming in their seats.

Teacher eye contact is crucial when a student is talking. It demonstrates that you are listening and interested in the conversation. Generally, when you or your students no longer want to continue a discussion, eye contact will be broken. Eye contact will be avoided when you or your students to not wish to recognize another person. When students do not wish to answer questions, they will avoid looking at you.

If you want to control minor behavioral disruptions, eye contact is the solution. When two children are whispering among themselves, direct eye contact from you will usually end the conversation. Your eye contact reminds students that your are aware of the activities taking place in the classroom.

Body Movements

Do you stand or sit when reading a story? Do you pace back and forth when explaining a science experiment? Do you use your hands to express your opinions? Body Movement can play an important role in conveying your meanings, feelings, or attitudes to your students. Many teachers discover that they spend so much time and energy trying to control their facial expressions that they are virtually unaware of what the rest of their body is doing.

Posture is one important aspect of body movement. Your posture can set the mood for the classroom. If you are too relaxed -- feet up on the desk, the body resembling a bowl of gelatin -- students will also be very relaxed. You may have a hard time administering assignments, projects, and general discipline. In the opposite direction, if your posture is too rigid -- straight up and down, soldier material -- students will also be rigid. You may find students adhering to assignments and rules, but not being able to relax or feel at ease in the classroom.

It's important to maintain good posture while teaching -- but be comfortable. Good posture can help vocal projection, control fatigue and eliminate back pain, while setting the tone of your classroom atmosphere.

Gestures or hand movements also play important roles in your communication. Gestures describe, regulate, and support verbal messages. (See **Activity 2**).

You can use your hands to point to a river on a geography map, show the difference between *big* and *large* or describe how a bird learns to fly. The easiest way to learn how important gestures are in your communication is to stop using them. Most teachers quickly discover that it is almost impossible to talk without the use of gestures.

The one problem you may experience with gestures is the tendency to overuse them. If students are paying more attention to your performance than the actual lesson, then you are probably overdoing it. Remember, gestures reinforce verbal communication -- they should

18

not distract from it.

Leg and arm movements also communicate messages to students. These movements should also support your verbal messages, not distract from them. Pacing, tapping feet, flapping arms, or crossing legs is distracting to young learners. Students will soon be watching your antics and spending more time counting how often you cross your arms in a ten minute period than paying attention to the lesson.

As a teacher be aware of your body movements while communicating with your children. Do the movements add or distract from learning?

Visual Aids

Blackboards, overhead projectors, maps, molding clay, and telescopes are all examples of visual aids. Visual aids can make an unique contribution to the communication process. Most children learn more readily when more than one medium is used. Visual aids can provide a wonderful extension of your communication skills if they are used properly.

In general, visual aids can help students recall experiences, correct faulty misconceptions, compare and contrast, demonstrate a process, stimulate interest, or raise further investigations. Photographs can compare the before and after devastation of an earthquake. A map can clarify how far away a city or a country is from the students' community. Planting seeds can spark interest in photosynthesis. Visual aids are tools to help you communicate information to your children.

Posters, blackboards, and bulletin boards must be visible for all students. Any material written on these aids should be short and simple. If there is too much information, it will be difficult for students to pay attention to only one item at a time. The use of colors on these aids should be vivid and simple. A good rule to follow is to use no more than three or four colors. If too many colors are present, they can distract a student's attention.

When using blackboards or similar aids it is important to maintain eye contact with your students and not to block their view. Give your students ample time to see all the material presented before erasing or moving on to the next idea. When finished with a visual aid put it away so children can focus on the new material. If you are going to use a pointer make sure you are talking and pointing to the same idea. Discussing one idea and pointing to another will only confuse your students.

If you are going to use a microscope, VCR, computer, or similar equipment, it is important to work with the aid before actual class time. You will waste time, become quickly frustrated and lose credibility with your young learners if you are unable to program the VCR or demonstrate a new program on the computer. If you are demonstrating the use of a visual aid (e.g., microscope or telescope) make sure all your children can see. After the demonstration ask if your students have any questions concerning the aid's use.

In general, make sure the visual aid has all its parts, the parts work, and you know how to use it. The visual aid is not the most important part of the lecture, but it will attract the most attention when it falls down, malfunctions, is missing pieces, or contains too much information.

Activities

1. Use the following nonverbal scale to evaluate your own or a fellow teacher's overall nonverbal communication skills. Mark the appropriate category.

Nonverbal Scale

	Needs Work	Average	Outstanding
Facial Expressions			
Expressiveness	_____	_____	_____
Mixed Signals	_____	_____	_____
Eye Contact			
Classroom	_____	_____	_____
Individual	_____	_____	_____
Body Movements			
Posture	_____	_____	_____
Gestures	_____	_____	_____
Arms & Legs	_____	_____	_____
Visual Aids	_____	_____	_____
Overall effectiveness	_____	_____	_____

After you have rated a teacher, can you give an example of a nonverbal communication skill that s/he does well? One s/he does poorly? On what one skill would you have her/him work?

2. The following exercises will help improve your use of gestures.

   A. Describe the following comparisons and contrasts:

      1. tall and short

      2. large and small

      3. square and round

      4. narrow and wide

What are other comparisons that can be described with gestures?

   B. Regulate the following actions only through the use of your hands.

      1. Stop

      2. Come

      3. Be quiet

      4. Listen

What other actions can you regulate with gestures?

C. Support the following statements with gestures.

1. The first point.

2. You need to move here.

3. Good answer.

4. Quiet down.

5. No.

What other statement can you support using gestures?

Story Delivery Skills

Stories can excite the imagination of young learners. For non-reading students, stories can initiate interest in books and for older students stories can increase the level of knowledge, appreciation, and respect for literature. Stories are an important part of the elementary school curriculum. Stories can contribute to young learners' overall academic growth. Reading or telling stories to students is not a passive process. When you have good story skills you can engage your students in a wide range of academic activities.

It is not difficult to develop good story skills. Reading or telling a story takes preparation and practice. Do my students stay interested in the story? Or are they restless and bored? Do I use good vocal inflection? Can all my students see the pictures in the book? When I tell a story is it organized? Or do I leave out parts of the plot? Do I use gestures? Can all my students hear me? Young learners enjoy listening to stories so the better your skills the more enjoyable the experience will be for them.

There are countless stories that young learners love to hear. Start your own collection of favorites. Library sales, used book stores, and garage sales are good places to buy children's books inexpensively. Keep an index file with the title, author, and short description of each story. Group stories by themes, events, holidays, characters, plots, or other categories. When, for example, you want Halloween stories the index file will provide easy access to a variety of possibilities.

To discover what you feel are good classroom story skills use the scale in **Activity 1** to evaluate the story skills of teachers you observe in their classrooms. Then honestly evaluate your own story skills.

How To Read A Story

Use the following steps to prepare a story to read to your students. Select a story that you enjoy. It will be easier to read and express your enthusiasm if you like the story.

First, pre-read your selection. Never read a story unprepared. Preparation eliminates mispronunciations, stumbling, loss of place, and poor delivery skills.

Second, read the story aloud several times. Listen for the rhythm and style of the story. Where is the climax? Is there use of rhyme? Is there dialogue? The rhythm and style of the story dictate the speed. If the characters are talking excitedly you will want to quicken your rate. The use of rhyme also requires a quicker pace. Use slash marks [//] to indicate where you want to pause. (See **Activity 2**). This will be a visual cue and will help the overall flow of the story.

Third, look for key phrases in the story. What words do you want to emphasize with vocal inflection? Underline [_____] those words to indicate vocal emphasis. (See **Activity 2**).

Fourth, plan gestures and body movements. What types of action can you incorporate into the story to bring it to life? Actions that are awkward and unnatural should be avoided.

Fifth, plan your introduction. How do you want to introduce this story to your students? You can use illustrations, rhetorical questions, examples, props; the possibilities are endless. Always state the title and author of the story.

Sixth, plan your conclusion. Your story should have a clear and concise ending. When you reach the last line close the book, look at your students, and in a slower rate of speed say the last line.

Seventh, if appropriate, decide if you will show the book's pictures. Some book's pictures are an important part of the overall theme; others are not. The pictures should be large enough so all your students can see them. Hold the book at a level that is comfortable for your students while giving them an ample amount of time to see each picture.

Eighth, practice, practice, practice! Good speaking skills are essential. Students should be able to hear and see you, your eyes focusing on them, as you incorporate good diction, vocal expressiveness, gestures and body movements into your reading. (See **Activity 3**).

Ninth, plan a pleasant reading environment. Set the stage for student listening, free from as many distractions as possible.

How To Tell A Story

Use the following steps to prepare a story to tell to your students. Select a story that you enjoy. It will be easier to tell and express your enthusiasm when you like the story.

First, pre-tell your selection. Never tell a story unprepared. Preparation eliminates mispronunciations, stumbling, loss of place, and poor delivery skills.

Second, outline the story for easier telling. Choose a story with a simple plot, limited characters, and action. The more complicated the story the more difficult it is to remember all the pieces. Look at the plot and climax of the story for keys to outlining the story.

Third, examine the characters of the story. How do they speak? How do they appear? How can you portray them?

Fourth, look for key phrases in the story. What words do you want to emphasize with vocal inflection?

Fifth, plan gestures and body movements. What types of action can you incorporate into the story to bring it to life? Actions that are awkward and unnatural should be avoided.

Sixth, tell your story aloud several times. Listen for the rhythm and style of the story. Is there a clear and effective organization to your story? Is there a beginning, middle, and end? How is your rate of speed? Are you talking too fast? Too slow?

Seventh, plan your introduction. How do you want to introduce this story to your students?

26

Do you need to explain the setting, scene, or characters? You can use illustrations, rhetorical questions, examples, props; the possibilities are endless. Always state the title and author of the story.

Eighth, plan your conclusion. Your story should have a clear and concise ending. Your rate of speed should be slower. Vocal projection should drop as you tell the conclusion.

Ninth, if appropriate, use props to tell the story. Puppets, flannel boards, student participation, the possibilities are endless. Props should be appropriate to the story, large enough so children can see, and not distract from the story.

Tenth, practice, practice, practice! Good speaking skills are essential. Students should be able to hear and see you, your eyes focusing on them, as you incorporate good diction, vocal expressiveness, gestures and body movements into your telling. (See **Activity 4**).

Eleventh, plan a pleasant telling environment. Set the stage for student listening, free from as many distractions as possible.

Activities

1. Use the following story scale to evaluate a fellow teacher's or your own overall story skills. Mark the appropriate category.

Story Scale

Needs Work Average Outstanding

Delivery

	Needs Work	Average	Outstanding
Eye Contact	_____	_____	_____
Body Movements	_____	_____	_____
Gestures	_____	_____	_____
Rate of Speed	_____	_____	_____
Vocal Projection	_____	_____	_____

Language

	Needs Work	Average	Outstanding
Clarity	_____	_____	_____
Pronunciation	_____	_____	_____
Vocal Inflection	_____	_____	_____

Content

	Needs Work	Average	Outstanding
Introduction	_____	_____	_____
Conclusion	_____	_____	_____
Clear Organization	_____	_____	_____
Use of Props	_____	_____	_____

Overall effectiveness   _____ _____ _____

After you have rated a teacher can you give an example of a story skill that s/he does well? One s/he does poorly? What one skill would you have her/him work on?

2. Read the following alphabet story. Pause at the slash marks to practice your rate of speed. Use more vocal expressiveness with the words that are underlined. Starting with the letter "K" mark the story where you feel changes of speed and vocal inflection are appropriate.

Alphabet Soup

A is for <u>Annie</u> // the <u>amazing</u>, adventurous, alligator.//

B is for <u>Beth</u> // the <u>bouncing</u>, brown bear.//

C is for <u>Carol</u> // the colorful, <u>cackling</u> cockateel.//

D is for <u>Douglas</u> //the <u>delightful</u>, dainty dinosaur.//

E is for <u>Edward</u> // the <u>enormous</u>, educated elephant.//

F is for <u>Flora</u> // the flighty, <u>flirtatious</u> firefly.//

G is for <u>Gregory</u> // the graciously <u>good-hearted</u> gorilla.//

H is for <u>Henry</u> // the <u>horribly, helpless</u> handyman.//

I is for <u>Ivan</u> // the icy, <u>impolite</u> icicle.//

J is for <u>Jordan</u> // the jovial, <u>jubilant jack-o-lantern</u>.//

K is for Kathy the kindly, knowledgeable kangaroo.

L is for Lauren the likeable, lemon lollipop.

M is for May the marvelous, magical monkey.

N is for Norma the naturally noisy neighbor.

O is for Octavia the occasionally odd ostrich.

P is for Peter the persnickety, pampered pirate.

Q is for Quentin the quivering, quizzical quail.

R is for Richard the red, raspy rhinoceros.

S is for Sheryl the sensible, stately scholar.

T is for Tim the terribly, tiny tailor.

U is for Ulysses the utterly useless unicorn.

V is for Viola the versatile, vibrating Victrola.

W is for Winslow the walloping, watchful walrus.

X is for Xenia the exciting, exquisite xylophone.

Z is for Zoe the zany, zestful zebra.

3. Read the following story. Mark it for appropriate speed and vocal effectiveness. Select gestures and body movements to add life to the story. Practice your introduction and conclusion. Practice your speaking skills.

What I Know

I'm on a trip

to the land of *Know*.

It's three steps east

and six below.

I jumped back twice

then took three turns.

I was almost there

from the map I learned.

I filled my pockets

with secrets and tales

Then raised the anchor

on the ship I sailed.

It had a captain's telescope

and prisoners making pleas.

The crew made all known pirates

walk the plank into the sea.

When the crew was getting hungry

wanting food by the pound

I sailed to the pepperoni islands

where trees bearing pizzas abound.

After the crew had eaten

I sailed off once more

The land of *Know* my destination

an unknown place to explore.

When the ship was docked

in the capitol of *Know*,

I visited King Know Nothing's court

and looked up my cousin Joe.

Then cousin Joe and I traveled

to Mount Limbo-loo

I marked our spot with his purple socks,

and named our claim, St. Knew.

King Know Nothing threw a party

inviting everyone well-known.

When all the guests had gathered

we started with what we had known.

The wisdom gained from our mountain adventures

we gave to all who came.

Knowledge is best when it is shared.

"To the great explorers," all proclaimed.

For the party's entertainment

Joe described the mountain tops.

I demonstrated my knowledge

describing travel plans, places and stops.

Many hands were raised and questions asked

seeking answers to things unknown.

The fun in learning is the discovery

the seeds of knowledge sown.

After my grand performance

I needed a good long rest.

So I headed back home, to my own backyard,

the place that I *know* best.

4. Outline the following story for telling. Remember the less complicated the story, the easier it will be to tell. Select key phrases that you feel are important to the story. Select gestures and body movements to add life to the story. Practice your introduction and conclusion. Practice your speaking skills.

My Sister's Monsters

My sister was afraid of the dark. She knew monsters lived in her closet. She knew they played with her toys and wore her sneakers. She knew the dustballs underneath her bed were lint from the monsters' belly buttons. My mom said there weren't any monsters living in her closet playing with her toys and wearing her sneakers. My sister said, "prove it" and my mom did.

My mom said, once, a long time ago, when fairies told tales, people lived in castles and cities were called kingdoms, a magician lived high atop a steep mountain. Below the mountain, nestled in a quiet valley, was a kingdom that the magician looked after.

Each morning the magician would conjure up the right amount of rain or sun for the kingdom's crops to grow. He made sure that on the first day of winter it snowed, and on the first day of spring, tulips and daffodils bloomed.

Now the magician had an apprentice. He had many duties including the task of collecting herbs and spices for the magician's spells. Before the apprentice was given the job he had to promise never, never, *never* to utter any of the magician's spells.

One day the magician received an urgent message from a queen of a far away kingdom. Her young son, the heir to her throne, had eaten poisonous brussels sprouts and was slowly dying. The queen needed the magician's powerful potions to save the young prince. The magician packed his magic herbs and spices and hurried off to save the young prince. Before he left he reminded the apprentice of his promise not to utter any magic spells.

During the first few days of the magician absence, the apprentice kept his promise and never,

never, *never* uttered a spell. But as days became weeks and the first day of Spring got closer and closer the apprentice began to worry.

What if the magician missed the first day of Spring? What if there were no tulips or daffodils? What would the kingdom think? Would they lose faith in the magician?

As the apprentice worried he began thumbing through one of the magician's magic books. He glanced carelessly over the spells coming upon an incantation he had never heard the magician repeat. The spell looked so unusual that the apprentice started to read the words aloud:

"High tide, low tide, sing to a silvery moon.

In tide, out tide, kings eat with golden spoons."

As soon as the apprentice said *spoons*, a mist rolled over the floor and monsters started to appear. There were monsters of different shapes and sizes and colors. Monsters came out of closets, underneath chairs, and through windows.

At first the apprentice was amazed at his spell. But he quickly discovered the kingdom was not amazed. The monsters were everywhere and the kingdom was afraid.

The apprentice pored over and over and over the magician's magic books for a spell to make the monsters disappear. But no matter what the apprentice tried the monsters stayed put.

As the apprentice started to go through the magic books one last time the magician returned. The magician went to put his magic bag in the closet but a monster had already placed his bags on the shelf and when he went to sit down in his favorite chair a monster was already relaxing there and when he went to look out the window down at his beloved kingdom another monster was blocking his view. The magician turned and looked suspiciously at the apprentice. The apprentice quickly told him about breaking his promise, the spell he had read, and the monsters he had created.

The magician shook his head, but he smiled. Without saying a word he went quickly to work mixing numerous herbs and spices. Finally the magician said:

"Fairy wings and magic rocks, tinker toys and building blocks;

Coloring books and baseball games, secret hideouts and stuffed bears tamed;

Chocolate cookies and pink bubble gum, circus tigers and tin soldier's drums;

With so much in your dreams this night, I know your nightmares will run in fright;

So snuggle in your bed with care, and know your nightmares are no longer there."

No sooner had the magician finished speaking than the monsters disappeared. They disappeared from closets and chairs and windows and the kingdom was no longer afraid. My sister thought this was a fine story, but she wanted to know where the monsters had gone. My mom said, "the magician could not make the monsters go away forever so he placed them in our dreams."

"Whenever you have a dream filled with monsters, remember, as soon as you open your eyes they will disappear. You will never find them playing with your toys and wearing your sneakers."

"What had happened to the magician's apprentice," my sister asked. "He learned to always keep his promises. After much practice, he learned to be a good magician and was rewarded with his own kingdom," mom said.

My sister no longer believes monsters live in her closet. The dustballs under her bed, she says, are dandelion fluff that fairies send their wishes on to far away lands.

Writing Skills

As a teacher, writing is one of your tools. It enables you to communicate your ideas to parents, administration, and other faculty members and they will form impressions of you from what you write.

Be sure your information actually needs to be in writing. Would a telephone call be more appropriate? Or a parent-teacher conference?

Concentrate on who will be reading your writing. Place yourself in the background. Tell the readers what they need to know, being explicit about anything you want them to do. Your writing should be clear and concise.

Before starting a letter or memo organize your thoughts. Jot down key ideas or work from an outline. Either approach will keep you focused on your objectives.

Do not overwrite. Make your meanings unmistakable. Avoid clutter. Fancy words such as qualifiers (e.g., really, very, pretty) or adjectives and adverbs cloud the issue. Omit needless words.

Use orthodox grammar and spelling. The word *through* is not spelled *thru* or *because* is not spelled *coz*. Look for your own common mistakes. How do you spell *alright, allright* or *all right*? It's *all right*, two separate words. Negative impressions can quickly result from a letter containing misspelled words or incorrect grammar.

It is not difficult to develop good writing skills. It just takes practice

How To Write Letters

Use the following steps to write a letter to parents, administration or other faculty members. Always check your school's policy for guidelines they may want you to follow and have an English handbook for any questions on grammar usage.

First, your letter should always be typed. Use unlined paper. Pastel colors or stationary with *cute* designs is not credible.

Second, the date and school address should be placed in the right hand corner. Your readers will be able to tell the date that you addressed the issue and where you can be reached. If you are writing to administrators or faculty, the address is not necessary.

Third, address your letter to the individuals you expect will take action based on your information. Use their correct names. With divorce, single parents, re-marriage and titles this can be tricky. Using Mr., Mrs., or Ms. and the last name is acceptable. Check the student's chart for clues.

Fourth, the body of your letter should be single spaced and double spaced between paragraphs.

Fifth, in closing your letter, Sincerely, Sincerely yours, or Regards are commonly accepted. Triple space before typing your name. In that space sign your name.

Sixth, if you are sending copies, at the bottom of your letter type C.C. and the names of those who will be receiving a copy. Always keep a copy for your records. For an example of a letter see **Example A**.

How To Write Memos

Use the following steps to write a memo to parents, administration or other faculty members. Always check your school's policy for guidelines they may want you to follow and have an English handbook for any questions on grammar usage.

First, a typed memo is preferred but a handwritten memo is acceptable if it is legible. Use unlined paper. Pastel colors or stationary with *cute* designs is not credible.

Second, the date should be placed in the right hand corner. Your readers will be able to tell the date that you addressed the issue.

Third, use a title line. This serves to draw attention to your central idea and can be used as a filing headline. Make your title direct, concise, and informative. Underline the title. A greeting or formal salutation is not used.

Fourth, keep the information in your memo brief, no more than three to four sentences. The body of your memo should be single spaced and double spaced between the date and body and your name and body.

Fifth, place your name at the lower left hand corner of the memo. If an address and phone number are necessary place these items after your name. A sign-off is not necessary. Always keep a copy for your records. For an example of a memo see **Example B.**

Examples

The following letter and memo can be used as a guideline.

A. Example Letter

Date
Schoolhouse
Schoolhouse Lane
City, State, Zip
Phone Number

Dear Mr. and Mrs. Parent,

This letter is to update you on Susan's progress in math. Two weeks have elapsed since Susan started working with the math tutor. During this time Susan's math scores have improved to a B-average.

I believe this strategy is helping Susan and would like her to continue working with the tutor. If you have any questions or concerns please call me at my home after five p.m.

Sincerely,

Mrs. Teacher

C.C. Math Tutor

B. Example Memo

Date

<u>Reminder: Teacher Faculty Meeting</u>

There will be a teacher faculty meeting Monday, January 3, 1991, at 4 p.m. in the faculty lounge. The adoption of new science textbooks will be discussed. Please bring your textbook recommendations to the meeting.

Mrs. Principal

Activities

1. List a one-word substitute for each of the following words.

   For example: very beautiful

   One-word substitutes: attractive, lovely, fair, handsome, ravishing

   very hard

   very easy

   very young

   very old

2. Keep written comments to parents as clear and concise as possible.

   Examples:

   Ed is a strong speller.
   Ed's spelling has improved this term.
   Ed still needs help from both you and me in spelling.

   Ed interacts well with his classmates.
   I am encouraging Ed to interact more with his classmates.

   Ed is pleasant to work with.
   Ed can be uncooperative in class work.

   Ed participates in class discussions.
   I am encouraging Ed to participate more in class discussions.

   Ed listens to directions carefully.
   Ed has difficulty following directions.

   Ed works well on independent assignments.
   Ed is easily distracted when working independently.

   Ed takes pride in his assignments.
   Ed need to take more time in proofreading his work.

   Write your own example comments.

3. Use positive, action words in your written comments.

 Examples:

does	builds	helps
can	shares	thinks
caring	gives	improve
helpful	understands	remembers

Write you own examples of positive, action words.

Addressing Communication

The following teacher's comments address the importance of communication skills in the classroom. As you read their comments think about your own definition of communication. What role will communication play in your classroom? How important do you believe good communication skills are to a successful classroom environment?

"Communication and education go hand in hand. One cannot teach effectively if communication is not a top priority. It is not how knowledgeable you are, what teaching techniques you use, or how much time you plan a lesson that is important. In the final analysis, communication between you and the students and the students and you, determines your effectiveness. The goal of teaching is to instill academic values and appreciation rather than amassing facts. You set the tone in both motivation and interpersonal relations and this is done through communication. Communication is not merely the ability to enunciate your ideas but also to understand the ideas and feelings of your students. Your goal should be to make sure every student has the opportunity to communicate. Before entering the classroom each day you should think of which students haven't had the opportunity to speak whether by your action or their choice. Then you structure your lesson so that you involve them in the communication process not necessarily by asking them questions but maybe by having them read or make some verbal response. Teaching is not just you communicating to an audience but making the audience an active part of the process."

Charles Heisroth, High School

"Probably the single most important aspect of communication a primary classroom teacher must employ is communicating with parents. This process can be divided into two parts: 1) General Communication, covering activities, goals, skills, general announcements, and classroom supply needs; 2) Personal Communication, individually informing parents of student progress. First, one cannot expect that all children can accurately inform their parents on what activities or lessons are covered each day in class. A weekly newsletter should review for parents' classroom activities including goals and objectives covered from the course of study as well as weekly announcements. Second, communicating a student's progress with parents through phone calls and individual conferences is vital. This is crucial when a child is encountering difficulties grasping key concepts, meeting behavior expectations or adapting socially to classroom cultures. Key to successfully communicating your concerns to parents, is reading parents' non-verbal cues. If parents are not open to listening you risk alienating them. This can result in not obtaining parent permission for further evaluation and delay special support services for the child.

The teacher needs to be sensitive to parents' reactions and openness to accepting the teacher's concerns regarding the child. Sometimes it takes several months, even years, before parents will permit special services or an evaluation to be administered. Sometimes kindergarten teachers must begin by 'planting the seeds' slowly regarding concerns. Careful documentation of student progress on a daily basis is necessary to help parents clearly see the need for such services. It is a delicate tightrope teachers walk, always focusing on obtaining the optimum learning environment for each child. It cannot be obtained without parent support."

Beth Jack, Kindergarten

"During my 50 years in the classroom, stretching from the 6th grade to those working on graduate degrees, I have increasingly recognized the absolute necessity at all levels for excellent communication skills by both teacher and the student. Communication is always a two-way street and unless both teacher and pupil react and respond appropriately to each other, no instruction or learning occurs. Fundamental to the development of this communication interchange is the need to know one's subject and possess the essential facts of the discipline,

45

coupled with attention-grabbing supplementary illustrative materials to make the subjects vital to every student. Pupils begin their schooling with an excited, eager desire to learn, but tragically, many lose that zeal somewhere during those early elementary years. Failure to capture and exploit that youthful enthusiasm must spring in large part from the teacher's inability to build a communication highway with students."

Paul Boase, University

"As a high school social studies teacher for the past thirteen years, I have learned much about my profession. In preparation, my undergraduate secondary education classes helped prepare me for the many possible pedagogical approaches in the classroom. My social studies courses further prepared me by giving me a thorough knowledge base. But, only through experience have I learned that the most important skill needed for effective teaching is the ability to communicate. I must communicate with teenagers, teaching peers, administrators and parents. Obviously, the range of ages and subcultures I interact with is extreme. But, the communication process remains the same, only the content of the conversation changes. No matter how knowledgeable I am about the content or how I vary the teaching strategies, only through good communication techniques will the content be learned. Students can voice their opinions in my classroom without fear of retribution. The best classes are filled with dialogue between teacher and student(s). When interacting with other teachers, administrators or parents, good communication skills are of paramount importance. On many occasions conflicts were avoided or my desires were met because of my ability to communicate. There are many ingredients needed for successful teaching. My experience has taught me that the most important one is the ability to communicate. Educational preparatory classes should emphasize communication skills more. The smartest teachers are often not the best teachers. Classroom learning is achieved when teachers can communicate well."

Tim Jack, High School

"Teaching is an interactive encounter with four goals: 1) to develop how to think and behave in a native culture; 2) to grow from the impatience of a child's expression to the patience of mature conceptual thought; 3) to learn to live in a symbolic world that grows from the immediate community to the community that encircles the world; 4) to appreciate the creativity of each human brain and soul that can free itself from the limitations of ignorance and socialization. To do this I must share with each human in my learning community not only an ego, but a soul with divine possibilities. I must recognize that teaching is an invitation to learn. I must recognize my own limitations so not to get in the way of the other learner. I cannot teach anyone anything; that is the secret to the process. I can invite through confrontation, through challenge, through care, and through dialogue. The wise teacher knows when to get out of the way. While I cannot teach anyone anything, I can impede and interrupt the learner. Teachers, if they are to complete their work, are destined to always be learners. We do not primarily teach so that students can get jobs. We teach so that learners can get lives, so they can think the world."

Ray Wagner, University

"My classroom consists of eight multi-handicapped students ranging from age 11-16, with IQ's from 80 and below, some with severe behavioral problems to typical behavioral problems of the low functioning population. Parents, in many cases, are functioning on a similar level of their child. Others are tired of fighting the system and still others are demanding more rights for their child. My goal when I receive a new student is to communicate to the parent(s) the importance of their involvement in their child's curriculum. I stress consistency, responsibility, positive self-image, positive attitude, and independence. After fourteen years of teaching, I have created a Communication Sheet listing the goals from each student's IEP, home work assignments, the behavioral level they are on, the grades they receive every day, messages not important to call home about, and an area for parent's signature. Any messages from parents are written on the back. These sheets are useful during conferences, pointing out the lack of involvement from home. My process of communicating is unique to the situation and does take time, but the sheets show the patterns of parental involvement allowing for quick reaction. Parents are always able to reach me on the phone at school whenever they deem necessary. I try to know as much about my students as I can, and through documentation and constant interaction with the parent(s), this form of communication has worked well."

Valerie Kinney, Multi-handicapped

"Being a professional clown, I had some real concerns about my classroom presence. I'm used to entertaining children and having them pay attention and enjoy themselves. But more important, the children usually like the clown and are more than willing to cooperate with me. Substitute teaching is not quite like clowning...When the sub walks in the classroom, heads turn and eye contact is made. Some students speak, some smile and others look surprised or roll their eyes. The sub quickly tries to assess the scene and immediately introduces herself. Her reaction can determine how the day goes. It is important for the sub to have open lines of communication. Authority must be established right from the beginning. Explain that *we* have a job to do and that is to cover the material on the lesson plan. When working with students individually use the Sandwich method: Praise, Criticize, Praise. It's important that they realize that you are aware of their good attempts as well as their mistakes. I remind students several times during the day, that this can be a good day for them or a bad day for them. It almost always depends on them. They can make good or bad choices concerning their school work and their behavior. Substitute teaching can be quite an experience. A good sub makes the best of the situation by utilizing good communication skills to gain rapport, maintain discipline, and accomplish the lessons' tasks."

Jane Ruminski, Substitute

"One of the first, of numerous, times that I became aware of the importance of communication was with a young friend who had a communication disorder. Words and ideas were effortlessly spoken by me; for him, communication followed a tortuous route of expression because of his stuttering. Initially, it was difficult for me to understand that communication was not an automatic, comfortable event that "just happens." Because of the vicarious pain that I shared with my friend, it was a natural decision for me to major in communication in college, and eventually specialize in communication disorders. Over the past thirty years of working with all types of communication disorders in clinical settings, I have valued my earlier communication studies because they have given me the important referent of "what is normal communication." I remember working with a person who had undergone a total laryngectomy, and he, who once depended on his communication skills for his profession, was now unable to speak. He taught me that communication is much more than the spoken word. Meaningful communications were shared with him and I never heard his voice or heard him articulate a vocalized word. In valuing communication, my clients have been my teachers. They have helped to broaden my concept of true communication."

Lewis Shupe, University

"Good teacher communication skills are important because children learn from words as well as actions. Student teachers need to remember that they are always communicating. Many times their gestures or facial expressions do not communicate the same message as their words. Eye contact with children is extremely important. If a child is talking and the student teacher is not looking a subtle message is being sent: What the child is saying is not important. I've also heard student teachers using incorrect grammar. Teaching grammatical rules is pointless if children hear the teacher using incorrect grammar. Being able to shape children's lives is a wonderful gift. All teachers need to be constantly aware of the tremendous influence they have on students' communication skills."

Julie Ray, Third Grade

Communication Model

The communication model presented on the next page is a visual representation of the interaction between teacher and student(s). The communication occurring can be either intentional or accidental. Teachers and students do not interact in social vacuums. Noise pervades the classroom and can interfere with the interaction.

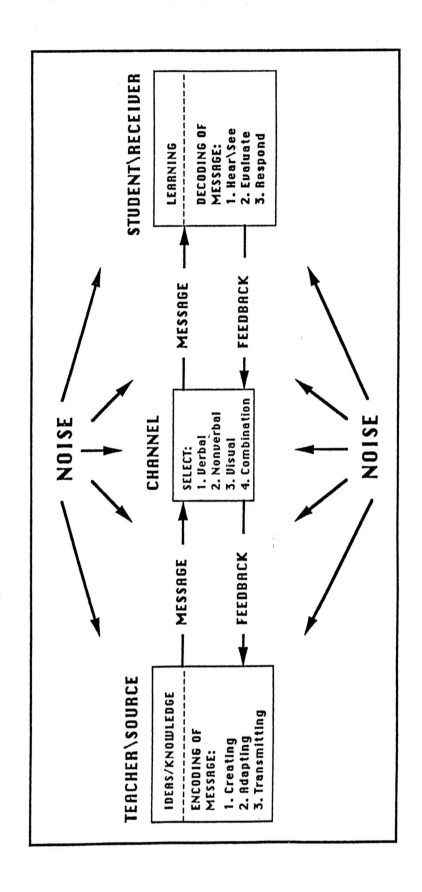

Communication Activities for Students

The following list of activities can help children learn to use their voice, body and facial expressions more effectively. These activities will also help children learn to organize their messages.

1. Describe concrete objects

2. Describe pictured objects

3. State name, address, parent(s) or guardian names, phone number

4. Read alphabet books

5. Read tongue twisters, limericks, rhymes, riddles, jokes

6. Finger plays

7. Show and Tell

8. Describe body movements

9. Pantomimes

10. Practice introductions, greetings, telephone usage (call emergency number or police for medical help, call a business and ask for information, answering and ending phone conversations)

11. Place a story in sequence

12. Story reading and/or story telling

13. Fill in the blank stories

14. Round Robin Stories

15. Picture stories

16. Speeches:

      autobiography

      weather or travel reports

informational (animals, current events, historical events, discoveries, disasters)

presenting solutions (math problems, science experiments)

famous persons (authors, scientists, composers, politicians, historical figures, artists, celebrities, sports figures)

book reports

newspaper reports

places (countries, cities, monuments, natural wonders, tourist attractions)

persuasive

17. Group Discussions

18. Debates

19. News Anchors/Reporting/Radio Announcing

20. Group Presentations

21. Analysis of a work of art (story, poem, play, movie, painting, sculpture, music, dance)

Minute Activities

The following activities only take minutes to complete. They are fun, easy to do and increase your students' communication skills.

1. Stories. These activities improve organization of messages, listening skills, story building skills, creative thinking skills.

A. Word At A Time

Each student contributes a word to the story. The story must make sense. Each student adds the next most logical word to the story. Students cannot use the words "and" or "but." Students can call out "period" to end the sentence then the next student starts a new sentence.

B. Class Members Story Completion

The teacher starts a story and uses a student's name in the story. Whose ever name is used must pick up the story. The story is completed when every student has been added to the story.

For example: It was an early Monday morning. The sun was bright and the air was warm. I looked out my window and to my surprise I saw _____ (student's name). You wouldn't believe what she was doing.

Look! It's _____ (student's name). What is she/he doing climbing that tree in her/his pink polka dot pajamas and red puddle jumpers.

C. Silly Stories

Make up a story and have students take turns adding to the story until everyone has a chance to contribute and then finish the story with the person who started it.

For example: The cow knew something "fishy" was going on. . .

I started hearing the strangest sounds. The cat was barking and the dog was mooing and the cow was. . .

Our teacher didn't come in from recess. We looked everywhere. The cafeteria, the library, and the principal's office. She/he wasn't anywhere. We decided to. . .

D. Story Bag

Take a large assortment of objects and place them in a bag that cannot be seen through. The objects could be ordinary objects (toothbrush, rock, coin, small toys, plastic animals, shells). The first student pulls out an object at random and starts to tell a story using the object. Each student takes a turn pulling out an object and integrating the object into the story.

E. History Of Things

Have students personify a "thing" (shoe, rubber band, sock) and tell its story. Each student must tell something about the "thing's" history. Where did it come from? Who had it last? Middle? First? How did end up in the classroom? Was it bought? Stolen? Borrowed? Lost? Found? How did it come to be? Nature? Man made? Did it have a purpose? Who used it? Animal? Human?

For example: Newspaper

The history: Where was it left? Who picked it up? Who read it? What section did she/he read? Who bought it? Where she/he buy it? How did it get to the place where it was sold? Who printed it? What articles were in it" Who wrote the articles? The history can continue all the way back to the trees in the forest that was used to make the paper.

F. Story Listening: The Big "**W**"

Ask students to listen carefully to a story. After the story is finished ask students simple questions concerning the basic facts of the story. Each question should start with a "**W**". For example: **Who** are the main characters in the story?

When did the story take place?

What was the main action taken by each character?

Where did the story take place?

2. Language. These activities improve critical thinking skills, listening skills, and vocabulary.

A. Object Description

Pass around an object (paper clips, feathers, apples). Each student must say one word to describe it. See how may times it can be passed around the classroom without repeating the words.

For example: Rock

Texture: hard, smooth, rough

Color: brown, white

Shape: round, flat, uneven

What can you do with it: throw, kick, hit, collect

Descriptions: stone, pebble, boulder, gravel

Type: limestone, granite

B. Word Alternatives

Give students a word and ask them to list as many alternative words as they can.

For example: Student

Alternatives: pupil, learner, scholar

Beautiful

Alternatives: cute, pretty, gorgeous, attractive, lovely, fair, handsome

C. Word Of The Week

Select an unusual or interesting word at the beginning of the week. Give students the definition and see how many times they can use it correctly in a sentence during the week.

For example: Cowcatcher

Definition: a metal frame on the front of a locomotive or streetcar to remove obstructions from the tracks.

D. Word Definitions

Select an unusual or interesting word and write it on the black board. Each student writes his/her definition of the word on a slip of paper. Definitions are read aloud. Students can vote on the definition they feel "fits" the word. The correct definition is then given.

3. Listening. These activities improve listening skills and critical thinking skills.

A. Riddles

Take a large assortment of riddles and place them in a bag/box.. Students take turn picking and reading the riddles to the class. Riddles can only be read once. The class tries to guess the riddles.

For example: Where does a sheep get a haircut?

At the baa-baa shop.

What happen to ducks that fly upside down?

They quack up.

What has four legs but can't walk?

A table.

B. Sounds

While students' eyes are closed make a variety of sounds. After each sound have students guess what the sound was.

Example sounds: clap hands, click fingers, ring bells, play flute/recorder, pound blocks, rub sandpaper together, flip pages in a book, shut book.

C. Object Drawing

Place an object in a bag. Select one student to look at the object for twenty seconds. Student then must describe the object to the class so the class can draw it. When the student is finished have her/him hold up the object so the class can compare it to their drawings.

Example objects: small toys, jewelry, plants, food items.

D. Word Drawing

Say a series of words and have students draw what you say. Only say the word once. Use words that could have multiple meanings and descriptions. Have students share their drawings with the class.

Example words:

rocking (possibilities include rocking chair, rocking horse, rocking motion) up (possibilities include arrow pointing up, elevator going up, mountain climber climbing mountain)

beat (possibilities include heart beating, musical note, vegetable)

E. Picture Drawing

Give a student a picture to describe to the class. This picture should be abstract containing simple shapes, letters, and numbers. Colors can be used if students have crayons or markers available. Students must draw that picture by following the instructions the student gives. When the description is finished have students compare drawings.

For example:

4. Nonverbal. These activities improve organization of messages.

A. Silent Interview

Tell students to work in pairs to find out as many things about each other as possible--hobbies, number of family members, favorite subject–but only by means of nonverbal movements. Give students a time limit (three to four minutes). At the end of the interview students should report to the class what they found out about their partners. Make sure students clear up any nonverbal movement misunderstandings.

Example movements:

sports: running in place (running), swinging a bat (baseball), hiking a football (football) hobbies: use hand movements to demonstrate sewing with a needle, painting a picture; use hand and feet movements to demonstrate karate, dance

family: show number of family members by number of fingers, swing arms back and forth with hands joined together to signify a baby in the family, point to yourself then to the finger that represents you in your family

B. Space Game

Make a large, square, circle or triangle on the floor with tape. Ask several students to enter the space one at a time. Have students discuss how and why students move to accommodate additional students into the space.

Example Questions: Why did students move? To accommodate others? Because they were uncomfortable? How many students in the space did it take to make students uncomfortable? How much space did students need to feel comfortable? If students were next to friends or someone they didn't know well, did that make a difference? What nonverbal behaviors did students demonstrate to show how (un)comfortable they were with the closeness?

Preparing for Parent/Teacher Conference

The parent/teacher conference is one way to include parents in their children's classroom experiences. The following outline will help you prepare for a successful conference.

Pre-Meeting Preparation

1. Parent Letter

    Include: where to park, class room number and location, time and length of conference, purpose of conference (general information, specific issues, get to know parents), possible questions parents might like to ask of you.

2. Teacher Preparation

    Collect materials that would be useful for parents to look at (current work, tests).

Conference (twenty to thirty minutes)

1. Opening: Make parents comfortable in "your" environment.

    Greet parents

        Welcome parents to your classroom.

        If appropriate introduce yourself.

        Tour of classroom.

        Overview of Conference

2. Discussion: Listen objectively to parents' concerns and questions.

    Student's progress

        Discuss positive and negative attributes.

        Present student's current work, student self-analysis form (see Activities).

Current Problems: Listen for potential conflict.

Determine probable causes.

Solicit possible solutions.

Agree on solution(s) that will be tried first.

Solution implementation (student, parents and teacher responsibilities).

3. Conference Conclusion: Wrap up the meeting on a positive note.

Brief summary of conference.

Choose a follow-up procedure (date and time).

Thank parents for attending the conference.

Activities

1. Student Self-Analysis Form

Name_____

1. My favorite work. . .

2. I sometimes need help with. . .

3. I feel_____has gone well.

4. What I like most about myself. . .

5. I could teach someone to. . .

6. I'm glad I learned to. . .

7. I'm most proud of. . .

8. I would like a lesson in. . .

9. My favorite subjects/activities are. . .

10. Four positive words to describe me are. . .

2. Role Playing

Think about how you would respond to each of these situations. Consider the parents', student's and your point of view.

A. A mother reports her son doesn't want to read the short stories that you have assigned because they are "out-dated" and "boring."

B. A father complains that his daughter was not selected for the basketball team because you don't like her, not because of her lack of ability.

C. A mother challenges your teaching methods. She believes her daughter would not be failing math if you would change your approach.

D. A father wants you to spend more time teaching science and less time teaching creative writing. He feels science is more important to his son's overall education.